Copyright © 2021 by Shanel Robinson

All rights reserved. No part of this journal may be reproduced or used in any manner without written permission of the copyright owner. For more information, address: mindyourmindcounseling@gmail.com

First paperback edition January 2022

Book design by Brittany Jones

ISBN 978-1-7378324-85
www.drshanelbrobinson.com

Don't get stuck in a
"moment in time"
for a lifetime.

Introduction

Let's face it. Life happens and it happens on a continuum.

When significant events happen, you are left with your thoughts, feelings and eventually your reaction. Depending on your interpretations and perceptions of the events you may develop helpful or unhelpful patterns of thinking, coping, and behaving. For these reasons, it is important to increase your awareness of how your thoughts, feelings, and behaviors work for or against you. Throughout this journal, you will work towards uncovering significant events that have had a long-term impact on your mode of thinking, feeling, and behaving. As you walk through these events, work to deepen your awareness of yourself and ascribe meaning to how your past informs your present.

Each week you will be given a broad overview of what will be the focus. As you go through the days you will deepen your awareness into yourself, your past, your present, and your future. Stay the course and follow each day exclusively (not jumping ahead), journaling specifically about what is asked.

Don't worry, each week you will have an opportunity to engage in stream of consciousness journaling in which you can allow your thoughts to flow. **Here you can write about ANYTHING.**

Now that you understand what lies ahead, when you're ready, get set, and GO!

Reflect & Release

Let the times you feel you have nothing, be an opportunity to figure out what you truly need.

Week One

Reflect & Release

For this first week spend some time exploring your early/significant memories. Consider the significant events, situations, circumstances, or changes that have impacted you. These events may bring up some negative and/or positive thoughts, emotions or feelings. It's okay. Allow yourself to take a journey to the past. We will take this slowly. Follow the prompts for each day as you gradually travel back to recollect important memories.

Think about it...

Week One
Day One

Reflect & Release

What memories come to mind about your childhood/early adolescence? Spend some time writing down the "what".

Example:
I remember when I went to go live with my aunt and her children during my parent's divorce.

POSITIVE

NEUTRAL

NEGATIVE

Week One
Day Two

Reflect & Release

Yesterday, you spent some time exploring the "what". Let's take it a step forward reflecting on what you were thinking then, versus how you see it now.

Example:
I remember thinking I didn't want to stay with my aunt and a lack of understanding why it was necessary.

POSITIVE

NEUTRAL

NEGATIVE

Week One
Day Three

Reflect & Release

Take a moment to think about the emotions and feelings you felt from the memories you've gathered. How do you remember feeling? Why do you think you felt this way?

Example:
I remember feeling betrayed and shut out.
I felt like what I wanted didn't matter.

I felt...

Because...

Week One
Day Four

Reflect & Release

Let's begin to identify any behaviors that developed from the thoughts and feelings you experienced regarding the situation(s) you described.

Example:
I found myself isolating from my everyone. I didn't want to discuss how I felt about my family falling apart.

Connect the thoughts that align with behaviors.

BEHAVIOR

BEHAVIOR

BEHAVIOR

Week One

Day Five

Reflect & Release

SELF CHECK-IN:

What did you learn about yourself from this week's exploration?

Week One
Day Six

Reflect & Release
Stream of Consciousness

Week One
Day Seven

Reflect & Release

Stream of Consciousness

> Don't allow others to project on to you, what's too heavy for them to carry themselves.

Week Two

Reflect & Release

This week you will begin to explore how the early experiences you recalled in Week 1 may be influencing your present. Sometimes we can relive past experiences in our waking lives. For example, some may find it difficult to develop attachments or connectedness with others out of fear they will be abandoned when/if something goes wrong. We can relive experiences such as these through our behaviors in relationships with others. This may happen for many reasons such as limited insight and awareness of the impact, lack of exploration, unresolved feelings, resentment, and suppression surrounding significant events

Think about it...

Week Two
Day One

Reflect & Release

What connections, if any, can you connect between the events listed in Week 1 and how it may appear in the present?

| EVENT | EVENT | EVENT | EVENT |

PRESENT CONNECTIONS

Week Two
Day Two

Reflect & Release

Spend some time reflecting on the connections you found. What are your thoughts?

POSITIVE

NEUTRAL

NEGATIVE

Notes

Week Two
Day Three

Reflect & Release

Let's begin to add in some feelings. What do you feel now that you have awareness that your past, in some ways, informed your present?

SINGLE WORDS

_____
_____
_____
_____

FULL THOUGHTS

Week Two
Day Four

Reflect & Release

How have your thoughts and feelings influenced your behaviors since the event?

BEHAVIOR

BEHAVIOR

BEHAVIOR

Notes

Week Two
Day Five

Reflect & Release

SELF CHECK-IN:

What did you learn about yourself from this week's exploration?

Week Two
Day Six

Reflect & Release
Stream of Consciousness

Week Two
Day Seven

Reflect & Release
Stream of Consciousness

> Your peace is precious, **protect it.**

Week Three

Reflect & Release

At this point, you've discovered somethings about yourself that you did not know before. Maybe you have discovered your upbringing has helped you to develop healthy boundaries and better awareness of yourself. You may have discovered your upbringing created unresolved feelings and unhelpful behavioral patterns. This week you will spend some time reflecting on what characteristics you've inherited. You can decide for yourself if these characteristics are helpful or harmful. You will spend time reflecting on the memories, their connection to the present, and how it has manifested.

Think about it...

Week Three — Day One

Reflect & Release

What characteristics have you inherited from your past knowingly and/or unknowingly?

POSITIVE

NEUTRAL

NEGATIVE

Week Three
Day Two

Reflect & Release

What are your thoughts about the characteristics you identified yesterday?

Week Three
Day Three

Reflect & Release

How do you feel about the characteristics you've inherited?

INHERITED

THOUGHTS & FEELINGS

Week Three
Day Four

Reflect & Release

How have your behaviors reflected your inheritance of the characteristics identified?

BEHAVIOR

BEHAVIOR

BEHAVIOR

INHERITED

REFLECTION

REFLECTION

REFLECTION

Notes

Week Three
Day Five

Reflect & Release

SELF CHECK-IN:

What did you learn about yourself from this week's exploration?

_____
_____
_____
_____
_____
_____
_____
_____
_____
_____
_____
_____
_____
_____
_____
_____
_____
_____
_____
_____
_____
_____
_____
_____

Week Three
Day Seven

Reflect & Release

Stream of Consciousness

> Dysfunction does not have to be your normal. Appreciate healthy and trash toxic.

Week Four

Reflect & Release

Yay! You made it to Week 4! It's not always easy rehashing the past. Commend yourself for the deep reflections you've done thus far! In this final week we will think about what you have identified you want to change or simply acknowledge. For some this may be a need to forgive or resolve lingering feelings from your past that continue to impact you adversely. For others, this may mean implementing gratitude and appreciation for what was instilled within you. For all, this means acknowledging that you have the tools within to maintain and/or reshape the narrative regardless of what the past or present has revealed, reflecting on how you will use your present to inform your future.

Think about it...

Week Four
Day One

Reflect & Release

Today, spend some time reflecting on what changes you would like to see within yourself based on what you have learned. If there are no changes, what do you need to acknowledge more in your daily life?

ACKNOWLEDGEMENT

CHANGE

Week Four
Day Two

Reflect & Release

What steps will you take to make these changes or acknowledge certain aspects of yourself that you didn't before?

GETTING STARTED ▶

MAINTAINING MOMENTUM ▶▶

LONG-TERM GOALS ▶▶▶

Week Four
Day Three

Reflect & Release

What are your thoughts and feelings about what you've listed?

_____
_____
_____
_____
_____
_____
_____
_____
_____
_____
_____
_____
_____
_____
_____
_____
_____
_____

Week Four
Day Four

Reflect & Release

What behaviors will you need to see from yourself to know these steps are positively impacting your future?

BEHAVIOR

_____
_____
_____
_____
_____

BEHAVIOR

_____
_____
_____
_____
_____

BEHAVIOR

_____
_____
_____
_____
_____

Week Four

Day Five

Reflect & Release

SELF CHECK-IN:

What did you learn about yourself from this week's exploration? Spend some time affirming the work you have managed to do throughout this journal.

AFFIRM

Week Four
Day Six

Reflect & Release

Stream of Consciousness

Week Four
Day Seven

Reflect & Release

Stream of Consciousness

> Stop letting people tell you how you feel, you said what you said.

Congratulations!

I am so proud of you for making it to the end of your journal. Just remember the journey doesn't stop here. Life will continue to happen, so make a commitment to stay in tune with yourself. After all, your experiences are influential and shape who you are.

Now with that being said,
never forget to REFLECT and RELEASE!

—Dr. Shanel Robinson

——— Reflect & Release

Copyright © 2021 by Shanel Robinson
ISBN: 978-1-7378324-85

www.ingramcontent.com/pod-product-compliance
Lightning Source LLC
Chambersburg PA
CBHW051258110526
44589CB00025B/2873